And this our life . . .
Finds tongues in trees, books in the running brooks,
Sermons in stones, and good in every thing.

AS YOU LIKE IT, II, 1

Here's flowers for you;
Hot lavender, mints,
savory, marjoram;
The marigold, that
goes to bed wi' the sun . . .
THE WINTER'S TALE, IV, 3

Here will we sit,
and let the sounds of music
creep in our ears.

THE MERCHANT OF VENICE, V, 1

We are such stuff
As dreams are made on; and our little life
Is rounded with a sleep.

THE TEMPEST, IV, 1

William Shakespeare
& the Globe

WRITTEN & ILLUSTRATED BY

ALIKI

HARPERCOLLINS*PUBLISHERS*

All the world's a stage,
And all the men and women merely players:
They have their exits and their entrances;
And one man in his time plays many parts.

AS YOU LIKE IT, II, 7

William Shakespeare & the Globe Copyright © 1999 by Aliki Brandenberg Printed in the U.S.A. All rights reserved. Visit us on the World Wide Web! www.harperchildrens.com
Library of Congress Cataloging-in-Publication Data   Aliki.   William Shakespeare & the Globe / written & illustrated by Aliki.   p.   cm.   Summary: Tells the story of the well-known playwright,
William Shakespeare, and of the famous Globe Theatre in which many of his works were performed. ISBN 0-06-027820-X. — ISBN 0-06-027821-8 (lib. bdg.) — ISBN 0-06-443722-1 (pbk.)   1. Shakespeare,
William, 1564–1616—Stage history—England—London—Juvenile literature.   2. Shakespeare, William, 1564–1616—Stage history—To 1625—Juvenile literature.   3. Globe Theatre (Southwark,
London, England)—Juvenile literature.   4. Theater—England—London—History—16th century—Juvenile literature.   5. Theaters—England—London—Reconstruction—Juvenile literature.
[1. Shakespeare, William, 1564–1616.   2. Authors, English.   3. Globe Theatre (Southwark, London, England).   4. Theaters—England—London.]   I. Title.   II. William Shakespeare and the Globe.
PR2920.A55   1999   98-7903   792'.09421'09031—DC21   CIP   AC   Typography by Al Cetta   ❖

Contents

Let us from point to point this story know,
To make the even truth in pleasure flow.

ALL'S WELL THAT ENDS WELL, V, 3

O wonderful, wonderful, and most wonderful wonderful!
and yet again wonderful,
and after that, out of all whooping!
AS YOU LIKE IT, III, 2

For Eileen Skeete Fiorentino

&

Al, Chris, Brian, Mark,
Susan, Sara, Janice,
Gregory, Diana, Jeffrey,
Anna,
Wesley, Mia, Alec—
Fiorentinos all.

Heartfelt thanks to many who are not listed here, and to those who are:
Ann Myers Liacouras, who said the magic words: "It's archaeology," Phoebe Yeh and
Al Cetta, who rode through the fire, Chantal Miller Schütz (Shakespeare's Globe), who
went far beyond, John Vitale and Lucille Schneider, who grant outrageous wishes,
Barbara Fenton for her eye and her wit, Zoe Wanamaker for her kindness, Franz for
always being there, Roxanne Kulakowski and Janet Carruth (Temple University),
Georgianna Ziegler (Folger Shakespeare Library), Renée Cafiero, Helen Chernikoff,
Kelly Rau, and April Jones for their backs and forths; the many authors and artists
whose books and drawings were devoured to create this one, and finally to Sam
Wanamaker, for his headlong, lifelong passion.

[ASIDE]

Though we read his works, quote his words,
and see his plays performed throughout the world,
William Shakespeare is a mystery.
Little is known about him—not even the exact day
he was born, or what he looked like.
What we do know comes from writings and drawings,
from records of christenings, marriages, and deaths,
from property deeds and wills.
We search for clues in the history of the sixteenth
and seventeenth centuries, in sites where he lived and died,
and we find some in his own plays and poems.
We have to guess the rest.

Reader, looke
Not on his Picture, but his Booke.
BEN JONSON,
THE FIRST FOLIO

WILLIAM SHAKESPEARE
1564–1616
Poet · Playwright · Actor · Gentleman

THE GLOBE
1599–1613 · 1614–1644
The "Wooden O" Playhouse

illiam Shakespeare.
Sooner or later, everyone learns that name.
It belongs to one of the greatest storytellers who ever lived.
Comedy, tragedy, history, fairy tales—Shakespeare wrote
about them all, in words that dance off the tongue.
We learn about the Globe, too—the playhouse where
Shakespeare's plays were performed by the greatest actors
of his time.

This is the story of Will Shakespeare and the Globe—
and the dream of a boy of our own time.
But more about that later.

Sam Wanamaker, the boy with a dream

*I'll note you
in my book of memory.*
HENRY VI, PART 1, II, 4

The River Avon flows through Stratford in the quiet countryside.

Act One

Scene 1

Will was born in Stratford-upon-Avon, England, more than four hundred years ago. He lived with his big family, crowded in a house on Henley Street.

John Shakespeare, a glove maker, and his wife, Mary, had 8 children: Will, Gilbert, Joan, Richard, Anne, and Edmund, and their first two, who died in infancy.

He went to the local grammar school, where he studied Latin, Greek, and subjects he would write about one day.

Will spent long days reading and memorizing drama, poetry, and history. His classmates were all boys, as girls did not go to grammar school in those days.

Anne Hathaway's Cottage

Mary Arden's House

Will's wife, Anne Hathaway, and his mother, Mary Arden, were both wealthy farmers' daughters.

When he was eighteen, Will married Anne Hathaway, who was eight years older. Anne joined the Shakespeare household, too.

The young family lived cramped in a bedroom.

Before long their daughter Susanna was born,
and then twins, Hamnet and Judith.
Now, with a bulging house and a new family to support,
young Will set off to find work in London.

The main road to London from Stratford is still over Clopton Bridge.

And so to the venture.
HENRY IV, PART 2, EPILOGUE

The hub of London life was London Bridge—a city unto itself. There were nearly 200 houses and shops on it, and even a church. Its narrow passageway was congested with animals, wagons, and crowds, and Will would join them, too.

Act Two

Scene 1

Ｌondon. There it was. A noisy, overcrowded city, built on the edge of a river—with only one way to walk across: London Bridge. Shoppers, traders, beggars, animals, and carts clattered along slippery cobblestone streets crammed with houses.

Busy London markets sold fish, meat, fruit, vegetables, and whatever people needed. But the crowded, unsanitary conditions and poor sewage attracted rats that spread diseases. Every few years a deadly plague broke out.

London Bridge was a marvel of its time. Over the centuries, it housed merchants and famous people.
It survived floods, fires, and rebuildings for 800 years, until it finally "fell down."

Boats and ships swarmed along the smelly,
polluted River Thames.
Barges hauled cargo to and fro, and wherries
rowed passengers across for a penny.
It was faster and easier than walking across the bridge.

Criminals were punished—sometimes with their lives. Rogues, thieves, and vagabonds were publicly whipped,
or clamped in pillories—as were vendors who overcharged or sold bad produce. Prisoners were jailed or executed
in the Tower of London nearby. Traitors' heads were exhibited on the gate to London Bridge.

I hold the world but as the world . . .
A stage, where every man must play a part.
THE MERCHANT OF VENICE, I, 1

15

ELIZABETH I
QUEEN OF ENGLAND

1534–1603

Poet · Musician · Linguist · Patron of the Arts

O queen of queens! how far dost thou excel,
No thought can think, nor tongue of mortal tell.
LOVE'S LABOUR'S LOST, IV, 3

Music was played and sung in houses, in churches, and on the stage.

Scene 2

Yet with the noise, smells, and sickness, there was music
in the air, and actors performing everywhere.
This was because Elizabeth I was Queen.
She cherished the arts.
She loved music, dance, poetry, and plays.
She encouraged the artists who created them,
and even invited them to the palace to entertain her court.
One day Will would be one of them.

Clowns, masked actors, and acrobats entertained and delighted audiences.

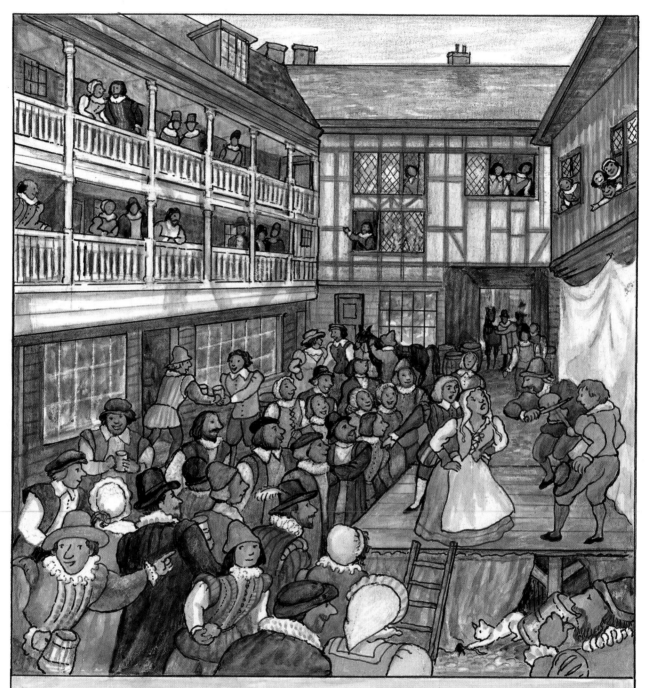

Actors set up their platform stage, hung a curtain backdrop, and performed on one side of a yard.
Visitors lodged at the inn could watch from galleries above. One such inn—the George—still survives.

Onlookers gathered in the road to watch wandering players perform.

In Elizabethan England plays were popular afternoon
entertainment among nobility and ordinary folk.
Locals and visitors flocked to see their favorite company
present a new play.
Traveling actors toured around London and the countryside.
They set up a stage and performed wherever they could—
in city or village inns and inn yards, or in wealthy summer residences.
Perhaps as a boy, Will saw them perform in Stratford
when they toured there.

*Also popular with the crowds was
the cruel sport of animal baiting.
In special arenas, bears or bulls
defended themselves from fierce dogs.
Cock fights took place in cockpits.*

The Bear Garden

*In spring-time, the only pretty ring-time,
When birds do sing, hey ding a ding, ding . . .*
AS YOU LIKE IT, V, 3

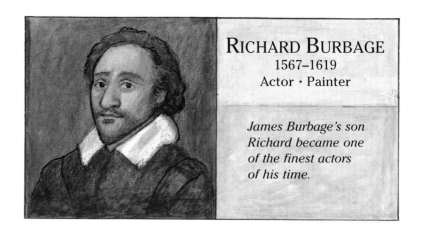

Scene 3

Traveling actors were not always respected
and were often treated like vagabonds.
One actor, James Burbage, decided that players needed a home
of their own to gain more dignity.
James leased land, assembled a company of actors, and built
the very first public playhouse in England.
It was called The Theatre—the name given to all playhouses after that.
The Theatre was a huge success, and by the time Will Shakespeare
arrived in London, more playhouses had sprung up.

The Theatre
1576

The Rose
1587

The Swan
1595

Early outdoor playhouses were modeled on animal-baiting arenas. They were circular, with a center platform stage and an open thatched roof. Each playhouse had its own playwright and its own acting company, named for its noble patron. One playhouse competed with another for its audience.

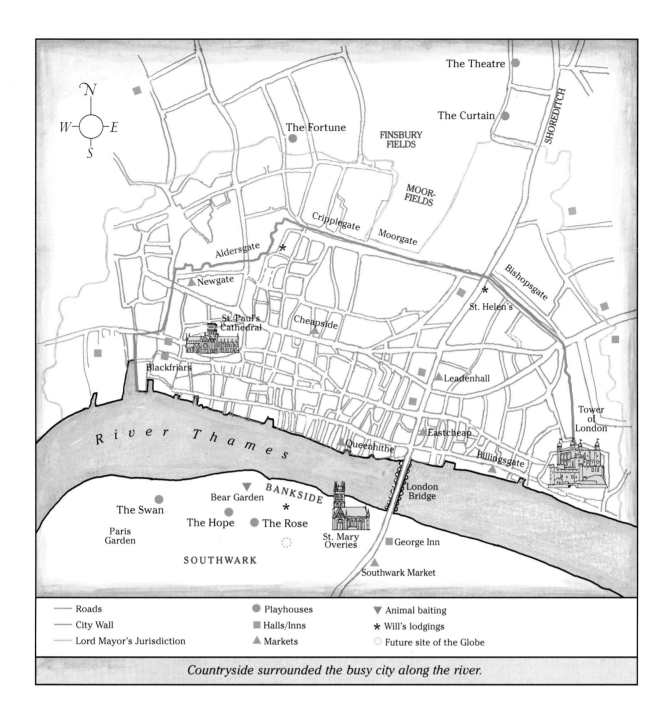

The Theatre

The Curtain

SHOREDITCH

The Fortune

FINSBURY FIELDS

MOOR-FIELDS

Cripplegate

Moorgate

Aldersgate

*

Bishopsgate

Newgate

*
St. Helen's

St. Paul's Cathedral

Cheapside

Blackfriars

Leadenhall

Tower of London

R i v e r   T h a m e s

Queenhithe

Eastcheap

Billingsgate

London Bridge

The Swan

Bear Garden

BANKSIDE

Paris Garden

The Hope

*

The Rose

St. Mary Overies

George Inn

SOUTHWARK

Southwark Market

⌇⌇⌇ Roads	● Playhouses	▼ Animal baiting
—— City Wall	■ Halls/Inns	✴ Will's lodgings
—— Lord Mayor's Jurisdiction	▲ Markets	⬭ Future site of the Globe

Countryside surrounded the busy city along the river.

Not everyone approved.
Though the Queen and her Privy Council backed the players,
the City Council and the Lord Mayor did not.
He said playhouses lured lazy apprentices from work,
and the noisy crowds attracted pickpockets and
too much drinking, and helped spread the plague.
The Puritans, a religious group, didn't like them either.
So playhouses had to be built in "liberties" outside the city walls.
Yet the play was the thing, and Will arrived in good time.

Out of this nettle, danger,
we pluck this flower, safety.
HENRY IV, PART I, II, 3

Act Three

Scene 1

No one knows when Will's interest in the theater world began,
or what he did when he first came to London.
Because of that, these are called the "lost years."
He eventually joined the Theatre as an actor and valued playwright.
Its new company, the Lord Chamberlain's Men,
was the best in London.
Will wrote parts in his plays with these actors in mind.

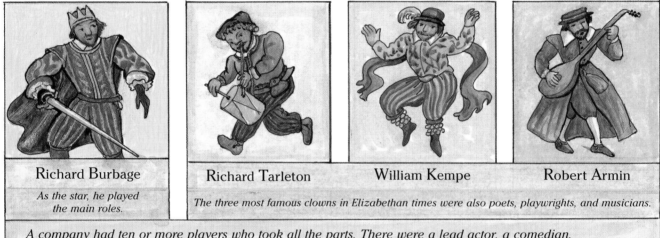

Richard Burbage

*As the star, he played
the main roles.*

Richard Tarleton   William Kempe   Robert Armin

The three most famous clowns in Elizabethan times were also poets, playwrights, and musicians.

*A company had ten or more players who took all the parts. There were a lead actor, a comedian,
and character actors who played kings or older men, as Will may have done.
Boys took the roles of women, because only men acted. Extra players and musicians were hired separately.*

Audiences loved Will's plays. They squeezed into the Theatre
with their food, drink, and rowdy chatter.

*The crowds bought nuts, apples, and pears to eat—or to throw, if they didn't like a performance.
And because water was dangerous to drink, many were tipsy with ale.*

CHRISTOPHER MARLOWE
1564–1593
Playwright

*The Rose playhouse,
where Marlowe was
the playwright,
was built by Philip Henslowe,
who kept detailed diaries
about his playhouse.
The diaries have helped
answer many questions
about the times.*

Over the river at the Rose were the company's rivals, the Admiral's Men.
They also had a brilliant playwright, Christopher Marlowe.
He was just Will's age and a great talent.
But when Marlowe was only twenty-nine, he was killed in a brawl.
After that there was no one to match Will's genius.
He wrote one brilliant play after another, and his company flourished.
Other companies performed Will's plays as well.

In his first nine years in London, Will wrote some sixteen plays packed with comedy, adventure, tragedy, romance, fairies, dangerous kings, brave heroes, and clever heroines.

Will wasted no time. In those two years he also wrote several plays.

Scene 2

A deadly plague interrupted the Theatre's success.
For two years all playhouses were closed.
People fell ill, and thousands died.
During this time Will wrote two long poems and dedicated them
to a dashing young nobleman, the Earl of Southampton.
The Earl was so honored, he became Will's patron.
Some say he paid Will generously.
By now Will was earning enough for his family to live in comfort.

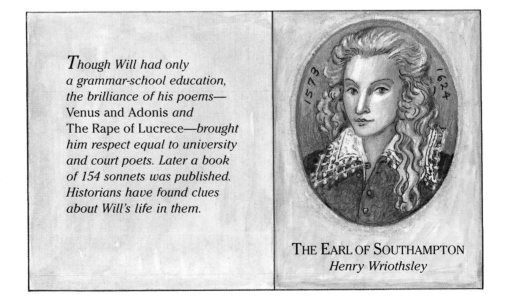

Though Will had only a grammar-school education, the brilliance of his poems— Venus and Adonis *and* The Rape of Lucrece—*brought him respect equal to university and court poets. Later a book of 154 sonnets was published. Historians have found clues about Will's life in them.*

THE EARL OF SOUTHAMPTON
Henry Wriothsley

The play's the thing
Wherein I'll catch the conscience of the king.

HAMLET, II, 2

Scene 3

For twenty-one years the Theatre prospered.
Then unexpected trouble hit when the landowner,
Giles Allen, refused to renew their lease.
He had other plans for the land.
James Burbage had recently died, and his sons, Richard
and Cuthbert, became managers.
For two years they pleaded with Allen while their homeless
company struggled in a rented playhouse, the Curtain.
Though Allen owned the land, they owned the Theatre,
and they wanted their valuable timber.
In desperation, the brothers decided to act.
They leased land across the river near the Rose, and waited
until Christmastime, when Allen was away.
At night they secretly began to dismantle the Theatre
and floated it across the Thames piece by piece.

With the timber they started to build a new playhouse.
And because all the world's a stage, they would call it the Globe.
By spring they were discovered—but it was too late.
Half the building was up.

Widow Burbage looked on as Peter Street, their builder-carpenter, led the brave team of twelve—including her sons. They started on 28 December 1598, and it took them nearly a month to complete the task.

*But screw your courage
to the sticking-place,
And we'll not fail.*
MACBETH, 1, 7

25

The raised flag—depicting Hercules shouldering the globe—announced the opening play. Perhaps it was Henry V. *An open-air playhouse like the Globe was for the summer months. In winter the company used an indoor playhouse, the Blackfriars.*

Act Four

Scene 1

By mid-1599 the Globe opened to instant success.
It was so popular, it soon drove the Rose company away
to build another playhouse.
Audiences packed into "the house with a thatched roof,"
sometimes three thousand at a time.
For sixpence the well-off sat in the Lords' Rooms to see—
and especially to be seen.
For threepence they sat on cushions in the Gentlemen's Rooms.
For twopence they perched less comfortably on gallery benches.
But most were "groundlings," who paid a penny to stand
in the yard beneath the open roof.
When it rained, they knew it.

Can this cockpit hold
The vasty fields of France? or may we cram
Within this wooden O the very casques
That did affright the air at Agincourt?
HENRY V, PROLOGUE

A Entrances
B Yard
C Groundlings
D Galleries (benches)
E Gentlemen's Rooms
F Two-penny Rooms
G Stage
H Heavens
I Hell (trap to below)
J Musicians' Gallery and Lords' Rooms
K Hut (contains cannon)
L Frons Scenae (stage wall)
M Tiring House/Dressing Rooms (backstage)
N Thatched Roof
O Raised flag shows play is on

Elizabethan playhouses had no scenery and few props. The glory of the Globe was the adornment of the stage—the richly painted Heavens, columns, and stage wall, and the hangings covering the central opening.
Special effects were provided by musicians and a stage cannon that shot blanks.
Often the elaborate costumes were discarded clothes—gifts from noblemen to their servants, who sold them to the company.

The Merry Wives of Windsor

Much Ado About Nothing

As You Like It

Henry V

Julius Caesar

Hamlet

Twelfth Night

Troilus and Cressida

All's Well That Ends Well

Measure for Measure

Othello

King Lear

Macbeth

Antony and Cleopatra

Coriolanus

Timon of Athens

Pericles

Cymbeline

The Winter's Tale

The Tempest

Henry VIII

*Will brings each character and every human experience to life with his wit
and the rich, beautiful language of his writing.
Elizabethans were critical and demanding.
They valued words more than scenery.
They used their imaginations to "see" the forests, seas, and battlefields in his plays.
They loved the melodious verse Will wrote. He was their bard.*

*Language was developing in Shakespeare's time, and has changed even more since then.
Yet we can understand the richness of his words; and without knowing it,
we use many of the almost two thousand expressions Will invented.*

*How many ages hence
Shall this our lofty scene be acted over
In states unborn and accents yet unknown!*
JULIUS CAESAR, III, 1

Scene 2

In the next twelve years Will wrote his greatest plays.

Some were sad years, and the dark, complex tragedies he wrote
reflected his mood.

Will's only son, Hamnet, died of illness at age eleven.

In 1603 the queen died and was succeeded by a new king, James I.

The success of Will's plays and the Globe—

of which he was a shareholder—made him a prosperous gentleman.

He bought his family New Place, the second-finest house in Stratford,

and invested in other properties.

He would soon move back to his family and the countryside for good.

Happiness surrounded New Place when Will's daughter Susanna married
Dr. John Hall and gave birth to Will's only granddaughter, Elizabeth.

Scene 3

Then disaster struck the Globe.
During a performance of *Henry VIII*, a spark from
the stage cannon accidentally set fire to the thatched roof.
In one blazing hour the glorious Globe
burned down to the ground.
Miraculously, everyone escaped unhurt.
It was a dark time for all.
Yet within a year a second Globe was built on the
original foundations.
It was even more glorious than the first, and its roof
was tile instead of thatch.
They weren't taking any chances.

Though one man's breeches did catch fire, a splash of ale saved the day.

*True is it that
we have seen better days.*
AS YOU LIKE IT, II, 7

31

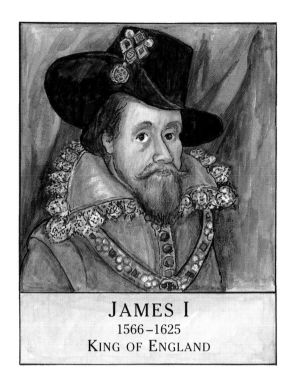

JAMES I
1566–1625
KING OF ENGLAND

*Costume design
by Inigo Jones
for Ben Jonson's*
Masque of Blackness

Scene 4

The London drama scene was changing, supported by the new King.
He enjoyed plays and entertainment even more than the Queen had.
He admired Will's players and became their patron.
They were called The King's Men and often performed at court.
At the Globe, Ben Jonson was delighting audiences with his plays,
and at court with his elaborate masques—musical dance-dramas.
Inigo Jones was designing a new kind of indoor playhouse
and creating lavish sets and costumes for the masques.

BEN JONSON
1572–1637
Playwright · Will's friend

INIGO JONES
1573–1652
Architect · Designer

*Inigo introduced the proscenium
arch—closed off with a curtain—
that we use today.*

*This must my comfort be,—
That sun that warms you here shall
shine on me. . . .*

RICHARD II, 1, 3

32

Scene 5

Will kept in touch with friends and events in London,
but it was time to rest.
In the quiet of Stratford, surrounded by the garden flowers
he had woven into his writing, he wrote his last plays.
A few years later, Will died on his fifty-second birthday.
He was buried in Holy Trinity Church.
As his friend Ben Jonson said:

He was not of an age, but for all time!

*"Shakespeare's Crab" shaded Will in life
and lived long afterward.*

Seven years after William Shakespeare died, actor friends
John Heminges and Henry Condell collected thirty-six
of his plays and published them as *The First Folio*.
But for that book, Will's work would be lost to us today.
Twenty years later, all playhouses were closed by the Puritans.
Eventually they were pulled down, and new buildings
covered all traces of the Globe.

Hundreds of years passed.
Then along came Sam Wanamaker.

Good night, sweet prince;
And flights of angels sing thee to thy rest!
HAMLET, V, 2

SAM WANAMAKER
1919–1993

Actor · Director · Visionary

Sam's lifelong link with Shakespeare and the Globe began during his boyhood in Chicago, where he was born. There, he saw a model of the famous English playhouse at the World's Fair of 1934. He would never forget it.
Two years later, his career as a Shakespearean actor and theater director began. His actress-wife, Charlotte, and their three daughters shared his life, and later his dream.

O brave new world,
That has such people in't!
THE TEMPEST, V, 1

Act Five

Scene 1

From the time Sam Wanamaker was a boy in America,
he longed to visit the Globe.
In 1949, when as a young actor he set off to live and work
in London, he thought his wish would come true.
But when Sam finally found the site,
all he saw was a forgotten plaque on a wall.

He was shocked that there was no greater tribute
to Shakespeare and his famous playhouse.
Sam became committed to an idea that became his dream.
He would find a way to rebuild the Globe as close to the original
as possible, where Shakespeare's plays would be performed
as they once were.

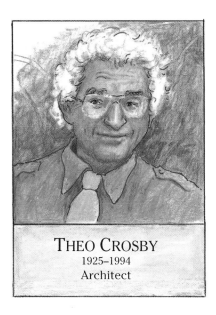

THEO CROSBY
1925–1994
Architect

Sam worked, talked, hoped, and pleaded until others joined him.
One of the first was Theo Crosby, who became the devoted
architect of the Globe.
Many others followed, fired by Sam's enthusiasm.
Experts studied drawings, letters, documents, and buildings
from Shakespeare's time, and found clues in his plays.
Sam and his supporters guessed where the Globe might
have been and would acquire land as close to it as possible.
They raised money, bit by bit, and then had to raise some more.
Then, by chance, builders digging at a nearby site
found the surprise of their lives.

Historians, archaeologists, and skilled craftsmen became involved. They sifted through often scant evidence to make their plans.

*We few, we happy few,
we band of brothers . . .*
HENRY V, IV, 3

Scene 2

There, buried near their own site, were the foundations
of the original Rose playhouse.
Later, they even found part of the Globe.
Now they could determine its size,
its shape, and how it was built.
These were the plans they followed.

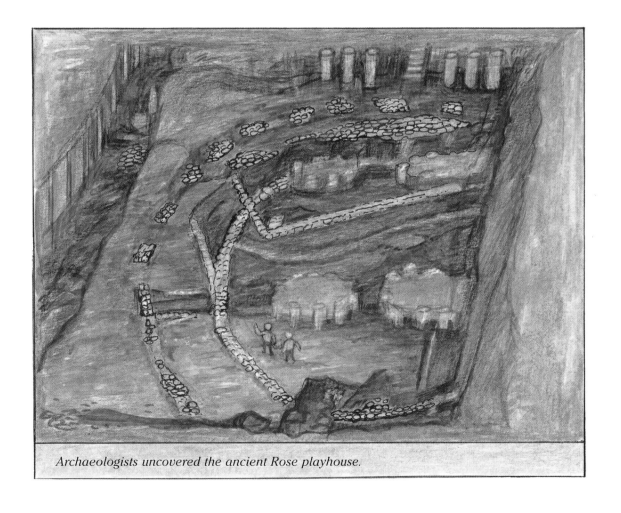

Archaeologists uncovered the ancient Rose playhouse.

What's past is prologue.
THE TEMPEST, II, 1

Scene 3

At last, work began.

July 1987, across the Thames from St. Paul's Cathedral

1000 forest oaks were donated.

They were handmade, based on Tudor bricks.

They dug the foundation,   chose the trees,   cut the timber,   fired the bricks,

Parts were made in a workshop, then reassembled on site.

Wooden pegs, not nails, held pieces together.

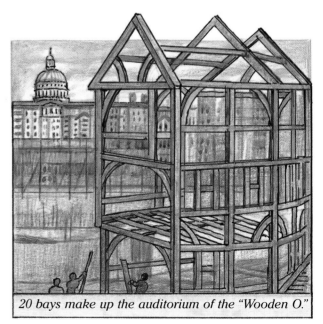

20 bays make up the auditorium of the "Wooden O."

joined the frame,   slotted the tenons,   assembled the bays,

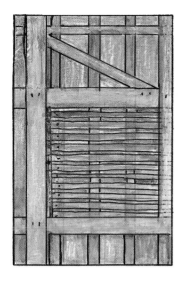   

Each baluster was made by hand.

attached the lathes,   plastered the walls,   cleaved the wood,   turned the balusters,

Suitable reeds came from Norfolk.
Thatching is an art that takes great skill.

The first and only thatched roof in London since 1666

collected the reeds,   thatched the roof,

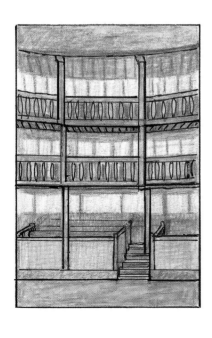  

In the center is a trap that leads to "Hell."

erected the galleries,   fitted the benches,   built the stage,

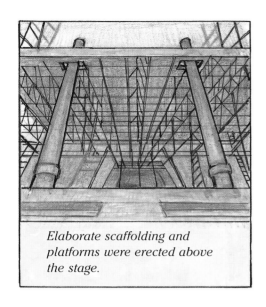

Elaborate scaffolding and platforms were erected above the stage.

This largest single timber in the Globe will rest on the posts that hold up the canopy.

Cement was covered with a mixture of sand, ashes, and hazelnut shells.

lifted the posts,   hoisted the beam,   covered the yard,

A central trap allows a god or a fairy to appear from the canopy space above.

raised the Heavens,

and added to the thatched roof what Will's Globe
never had—a sprinkler system.

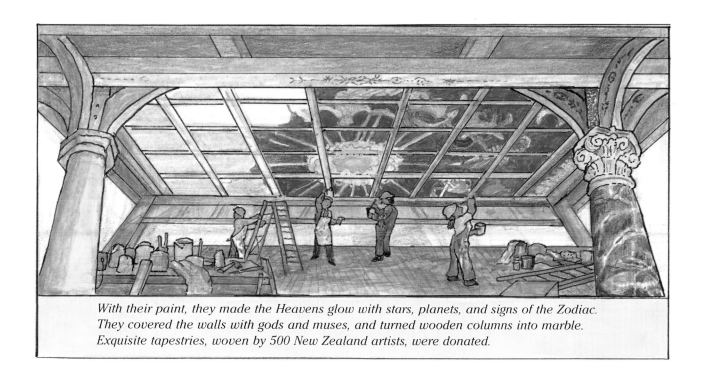

With their paint, they made the Heavens glow with stars, planets, and signs of the Zodiac.
They covered the walls with gods and muses, and turned wooden columns into marble.
Exquisite tapestries, woven by 500 New Zealand artists, were donated.

Last came the artists, with their paints and gilt, to transform
the stage into the glory of an Elizabethan playhouse.

And for the entrance, 116 artists from around the world
wove magic into the iron gates.
Each animal, insect, or flower they created represents
a quotation from Shakespeare's plays.
The new Globe was finally ready to open its doors.

The wheel is come full circle.
KING LEAR, V, 3

Scene 4

After nearly thirty years of dedication, disappointments,
high hopes, and the devotion of many supporters,
Sam's Globe finally opened.
Fanfare, fireworks, and a festival of celebrations,
attended by Queen Elizabeth II, burst forth
in a fortnight of nightly revels.
There was sadness, too, for Sam did not live to see it.

Yet Sam is there.
He lives on in the Globe playhouse he dreamed for us,
just as Will lives on in his immortal plays.

Sea-nymphs hourly ring his knell:
Hark! now I hear them,—Ding-dong, bell.
THE TEMPEST, I, 2

The Globe company of actors and musicians presented Shakespeare's Henry V *at the opening, 12 June 1997. Sam's wife and Theo Crosby were also missed that night, for they did not live to see it.*

Not.
The End
THE BEGINNING

*O, here
Will I set up my everlasting rest.*
ROMEO AND JULIET, V, 3

SHAKESPEARE'S WORKS

There's rosemary, that's for remembrance . . .
HAMLET, IV, 5

The Plays

1589–90	*Henry VI*, Part 1	1599	*As You Like It*
1590–91	*Henry VI*, Part 2	1599	*Henry V*
1590–91	*Henry VI*, Part 3	1599	*Julius Caesar*
1590–94	*The Taming of the Shrew*	1600–01	*Hamlet*
1592	*Richard III*	1600–01	*Twelfth Night*
1592–94	*The Comedy of Errors*	1601–02	*Troilus and Cressida*
1593–94	*Titus Andronicus*	1602–03	*All's Well That Ends Well*
1594	*The Two Gentlemen of Verona*	1604	*Measure for Measure*
1594–96	*King John*	1604	*Othello*
1595	*Love's Labour's Lost*	1604–05	*King Lear*
1595	*Richard II*	1606	*Macbeth*
1595–96	*Romeo and Juliet*	1606–07	*Antony and Cleopatra*
1595–96	*A Midsummer Night's Dream*	1607–08	*Coriolanus*
1596–97	*The Merchant of Venice*	1607–08	*Timon of Athens*
1596–97	*Henry IV*, Part 1	1607–08	*Pericles*
1597	*The Merry Wives of Windsor*	1609–10	*Cymbeline*
1598	*Henry IV*, Part 2	1610–11	*The Winter's Tale*
1598	*Much Ado About Nothing*	1611	*The Tempest*
		1613	*Henry VIII*

The Poems

1592	*Venus and Adonis*
1592–96	*The Sonnets* (154 of them)
1594	*The Rape of Lucrece*
1599 ▲	*The Passionate Pilgrim*
1601	*The Phoenix and the Turtle*
1609 ✳	*A Lover's Complaint*

▲ Date of publication of the second edition
✳ Date of publication

*. . . tragedy, comedy,
history, pastoral,
pastoral-comical,
historical-pastoral,
tragical-historical,
tragical-comical-historical-
pastoral . . . or poem unlimited.*
HAMLET, II, 2

CHRONOLOGY

and there is pansies, that's for thoughts.

HAMLET, IV, 5

1564	Will born April (some guess 23rd) / Christened 26 April
1564	Christopher Marlowe born (d. 1593)
1572	Ben Jonson born (d. 1637)
1576	The Theatre built (Shoreditch)
1577	The Curtain built (Shoreditch)
1582	Will marries Anne Hathaway (1556–1623)
1583	Daughter Susanna born (d. 1649)
1585	Twins Hamnet (d. 1596) and Judith (d. 1662) born
1587	Will to London? / The Rose built (Bankside)
1592	The Plague / Playhouses closed for two years
1594	Lord Chamberlain's Men formed (formerly Lord Strange's Men)
1595	The Swan built (Paris Garden)
1597	Will buys New Place (Stratford) / James Burbage dies (b. 1531)
1599	Globe built (Bankside)
1601	Will's father dies (b. before 1530)
1603	Queen Elizabeth I dies (b. 1534) / James I (1566–1625) succeeds her
1608	Will leaves for Stratford? / Will's mother dies (b. 1540)
1608	Granddaughter Elizabeth born (d. 1670)
1613	Globe burns down (29 June)
1614	Globe II opens / The Hope built (Bankside)
1616	Will signs his will (25 March) / Will dies (23 April)
1623	*The First Folio* published
1949	Sam Wanamaker to London
1988	Groundbreaking for new Globe (International Shakespeare Day, 23 April)
1989	Remains of Rose and Globe discovered
1993	Sam dies (b. 1919)
1994	Theo Crosby dies (b. 1925)
1997	The new Globe opens (12 June)
1999	400th anniversary of first Globe playhouse

Thereby to see the minutes how they run,—
How many makes the hour full complete;
How many hours brings about the day;
How many days will finish up the year;
How many years a mortal man may live.

HENRY VI, PART 3, II, 5

Words & Expressions

Shakespeare invented some 2000 words and expressions.
We use many of them without even knowing it. Here are some of them.

mountaineer	schoolboy	shooting star	alligator
fortune-teller	football	moonbeam	critic
bandit	bump	dew-drop	lady-bird
employer	worm hole	glow	luggage
manager	anchovies	radiance	eyeball
watch-dog	fair play	dawn	love-letter
	horn-book		

mimic	farm-house	gloomy	blushing
partner	bed-room	useless	dauntless
zany	birth-place	quarrelsome	soft-hearted
excitement	fairy land	fretful	motionless
shudder	lonely	worthless	noiseless
puppy-dog			

to elbow	long-legged	flea-bitten	upstairs
to outgrow	pale-faced	green-eyed	downstairs
to hurry	hot-blooded	snail-paced	forward
to blanket	well-behaved	never-ending	lower
to cake	successful	full grown	far-off
		laughable	

howl jig silliness leap-frog

Every inch a king
Pomp and circumstance
A tower of strength
Too much of a good thing

Wild-goose chase
Swift as a shadow
Bated breath
One fell swoop

Double, double toil and trouble
The crack of doom
Not budge an inch
To be or not to be
Rue the hour

For goodness' sake
A sorry sight
It beggared all description
To thine own self be true
There's the rub

In my mind's eye
In my heart of hearts
A dish fit for the gods
The milk of human kindness
The be-all and the end-all

Sweets to the sweet
Eaten me out of house and home
Neither rhyme nor reason
We have seen better days
Good riddance

What the dickens! Puke! Puh! Hush. Tut, tut.

Speak the speech, I pray you,
as I pronounced it to you,
trippingly on the tongue.

HAMLET, III, 2

47

SITES TO VISIT

I know a bank where the wild thyme blows,
Where oxlips and the nodding violet grows.
A MIDSUMMER NIGHT'S DREAM, II, 1

*M*any *of the sites in and around London and Stratford-upon-Avon*
mentioned in this book are open to visitors.

IN LONDON:
Shakespeare's Globe
Bankside Walk
Globe Playhouse plaque
St. Mary Overies (Southwark Cathedral)
St. Paul's Cathedral
Tower of London
Rose Playhouse (foundation)
George Inn

IN STRATFORD-UPON-AVON:
Shakespeare's Birthplace, Henley Street
Anne Hathaway's Cottage, Shottery
Mary Arden's House, Wilmcote
Hall's Croft, house of Susanna and Dr. John Hall
Gardens in site of New Place
Guild Church and Grammar School
Holy Trinity Church
Clopton Bridge

Good night, good night! parting is such sweet sorrow,
That I shall say good night till it be morrow.
ROMEO AND JULIET, II, 1